Bobby "Boogaloo" Watts

CHAMPION
without a Crown

Book Designer: s . a . m .

To order additional copies of this book, contact:
Xlibris
844-714-8691
www.Xlibris.com
Orders@Xlibris.com

ISBN: Softcover   978-1-4257-5015-2
        EBook   978-1-6698-0530-4

Print information available on the last page

Rev. date: 12/30/2021

THE BOBBY "BOOGALOO" WATTS STORY

SESSION I: October 21, 2006

I was born in Sumpter, South Carolina on 11/11/1949. I was born to Clarence and Corrine Watts. It was six boys and three girls. I am the fourth oldest child. I was born by a midwife in a house, something similar to a barn. That's how it was back in them days. I attended Rafton Creek Junior High School for two years and after that moved to Philadelphia with my Momma and my Pop. They got tired of being sharecroppers and they figured they'd move up to Philly to start a better life. I picked cotton, chopped cotton, pulled weeds and stacked peanuts and corn. I did it all between the ages of 7 to 10 years old until I came to Philly at the age of ten. When we got to Philly our first house was at 24th and Seybert Street and from there we moved to 20th and Brown and after 20th and Brown we moved back to 20th and Ingersoll. I attended Reynolds Elementary from the 3rd grade to the 6th grade. In 1963, I attended 7th grade at Vaux Jr. High School.

Life in the country was hard work, but I liked it. I like the country living. It is different. After being in Philly for a while I got home sick because I missed running around in the woods, doing the barn work and walking around with no shoes on my feet. Things like that you miss. You miss that country living. And then after coming up here in the city it was nothing like the fields. Right away I noticed the different houses and the jitterbugs hanging around the streets and on the corners. This really made me home sick because I wasn't in the wilderness. You couldn't walk wherever you wanted because of the cars here. It was a big difference between the country living and the city living. The way they live is different.

Bobby Watts (Boogaloo)

Bobby (Boogaloo) Watts Philas Top Middleweight will be coming to Wagner's soon.

After we moved to Philadelphia about a year or so later, my father passed away. He used to do a little drinking and he went to sit down on the front steps at 20th and Brown and he fell asleep. He fell off the steps and hit his head. He never woke up. They say he died from a severe concussion.

I used to look at the Friday night fights that used to come on television. I remember the fights at Madison Square Garden, advertisements for Gillette razor and John Briscendo was the ring announcer. I remember watching Benny K. Barrett get killed in the ring. My cousin Jimmy Young was the one who got me started in boxing in 1963. I was in the 7th grade. Jimmy became a heavyweight from Philly. One day I was in the schoolyard playing a little ball and he was on his way to the gym and I asked him where was he going. He told me he was going to the PAL gym on 22nd and Cecil B. Moore and asked me to come along. I thought about it and it sounded like a good idea even though I recalled being mugged a couple of times and Jimmy had his radio taken from him. This is what got him started and I joined up too. The jitterbugs used to ask me for money and sucker punch me in the head. They were the neighborhood bullies. I went to the gym for a couple of weeks or so because the jitterbugs were everywhere. If you went up a block or went down this block, or around the corner they were there. You were practically surrounded by them. You had to be able to hold your own. I wanted to be able to walk the streets and take care of myself. So by me going to the gym, I started getting a lot of respect. I remember a few times my brother was chased home by some of the neighborhood gang members. When I went to the door and they seen me, I noticed they turned around. So right away I knew I was getting respect from them because they knew I was in training. This was the beginning of my boxing career. I remember fighting in the amateurs. I remember my first fight where I won my first trophy. I fought amateur from 1963 to 1969 and turned pro in March of 1969. I had a trainer who was with me from the beginning. Jimmy introduced me to Frank Hamilton who trained me and Jimmy at the same time. I was also playing ball. "What kind of ball?"

From 1963 to 1969 I won just about every championship there was. My record during amateur was 45 wins and 3 losses. I won the AAU, The Golden Gloves and The Middle Atlantic championships. I went to the 1968 Olympic trials. I was the alternate to go to Mexico along with George Foreman and all the big joint fighters. But, I lost in the finals. This loss actually made me more dedicated to fighting. I was a sore loser. I thought next time around it wouldn't be a loss because I intended to win my next fight. It was a let down because I was looking forward to a gold medal and then when I lost it kind of broke my heart so it just made me work even harder. I'm the type of guy that whatever I participated in, I wanted to be outstanding and victorious. I always wanted to be a winner. I knew that I had more to give and I wasn't going to give up that easy. I couldn't take a loss easily. I remember even as a kid working in the fields, how my parents were always being told that they had a smart little son. I was always active, energized and a motivator. I was never a lazy type kid and always gave my all in whatever I did.

In March of 1969 I became Pro. I had gotten a last minute notice to appear in Baltimore, Maryland to fight Teddy Cooper who was fighting about 4 rounds at that time. It was about 1,500 people there to see the fight. The fight was held at a place that appeared to be somewhat of a catering place, something similar to the Blue Horizon in Philadelphia. I won the fight with Teddy by split decision. We went the whole six rounds. Teddy was a good, smart fighter, but the one thing I had in the back of my head was winning. When the bell would ring I went in with the attitude that I'm not giving up until it's over. The fight didn't seem as hard as I thought it would be by going 6 rounds because this was my 5th time doing 6 rounds. By the end of the 6th round I said "hey six rounds came fast I could have gone 2 or 3 more rounds. I thought he had an advantage over me by having three or four fights prior to our fight and he was my first pro fight. I felt really good. I had finally graduated to the next level. I said to myself, "Wow I'm a Pro now." I never fought a four rounder.

I started off with six rounds. I was paid $100.00 for fighting six rounds. I had also won about 8 six round fights. Three were fought at the Blue Horizon in Philadelphia. Two in Baltimore, Maryland, one in Washington, D.C, two in Las Vegas and 1 in Los Angeles. I lost the fight in Los Angeles to Armando Eunice.

After that, my trainer and I decided to go out West to start fresh with my career. On our way to Los Angeles we got stranded in Wichita, Kansas. Our car had broken down so we had to get it fixed. We had to call home for funds so we could continue on with our journey. We slept in the car for about two days until we received the money from home. After the car was fixed, I sold my tape player to get a couple of dollars for traveling expenses for the duration of the ride to Los Angeles. We finally made it to Los Angeles and once we were settled, we went to the Main Street Gym in downtown Los Angeles and began training there. I saw other great fighters like Ken Norton, Jerry and Mike Quarterly out there fighting and training.

During the time when I was fighting, I liked the game, the business and I loved boxing. It wasn't exactly what you would call fighting for the money; it was for the love of the sport. The difference with today's fighters and yesteryears fighters, in my opinion is that the majority of the fighters back loved the sport of boxing more. Today, it seems as if they love the money more than the love of the sport. I think it was more fighters that loved it because it gave them activities and an offer of an opportunity. It is a big change today than what it was back then. Back then, it was less opportunity for the fighters and now they have so many different types of activities or boxing avenues that they can get into so maybe that is part of the reason why you have less skilled fighters than you have skilled fighters. Today they are mixing the sport up with so many other opportunities out there.

PHILLY BOXING HISTORY — Boxer - Bobby Watt

| Home | Boxers | Fights | Arenas | Non-Boxers | Gyms | Relics | More | About | Contac |

RECORD

BIO

PHOTOS

NEWS

RELICS

EXTRAS

BOBBY WATTS

Bobby Watts

"Boogaloo"

38-7-1 / 20 KO

North Philly - Middleweight

Perhaps the most skilled of the 70's Philly middles, the longtime top-10 contender never climbed past journeyman status due to a weak chin. Was the first to beat Hagler.

Born: 11/11/49

"If I knew then what I know now, I would've been middleweight champion."

The Contender is good for kids trying to make it to the top by having good exposure, but then when you say Top Contender, they don't even compare to the Top Contender back in the day. The skills of some of today's' fighters and watching the "Contender" reality television show reminds me of the economy where you pay more and get less. You're paying them more money to box and getting less fight for your dollar.

I was the type of fighter that filled in a lot for other fighters that would pull out. They would call me and I would accept the fight. Sometimes, I would only have 3 or 4 days, a week, or at the most 11 days for another fight to prepare. This was how my professional career started out. I had a trainer but I didn't have a manager. I looked up to him as my manager. He was like my guardian while we were away. The manager dictates the fights for his fighter. I didn't have that. I was what you would call a free agent.

My biggest win came when I fought and beat the North American champ. His name was Ralph Palliton. He was out of Maryland. He was the number one in the world. He was the North American champ and he held a belt in which he never put up. I fought him three times back to back and he never put his belt up once. I beat him the first time, second time was a draw, the third time I stopped him by TKO in the 5th round. When I fought him the second time when the decision was a draw, I beat him worse than I beat him the first fight. He would soon be moving on to fight for the world title so he had to beat me in order to go for the world title. I stated at that time to the judges and referee that I wasn't treated fair. Especially, pertaining to the draw when I beat him worse than I did the first time. I also said to them, "Well, I'm not going to worry about it this time, because I brought my own judges and reparations. Originally, I was supposed to be an opponent for him the first fight. He used me as a tune-up. If he beat me than he could move on to fight for the world title. All the while, he never put up his belt. That's how it was. I had beaten six or seven Continental titleholders but I never got the opportunity to fight them for their belt. I fought the Canadian champ, and the New Jersey champ. I fought them all, but they would never put up their title. I fought Ralph Palliton who was the North American champion in December of 1971. Casey Gasey in 1978 who was the Canadian champ and Mario Roso in 1973 who was the New Jersey State champ.

James Marshall was the number one Top Contender. I fought all of these fighters and they never put up their belts. They were leery of taking chances with me because if they fought me and lost the fight they would lose their title so they never put up their title. No matter what the outcome of the fight or title won or lost, I just went into the ring fought a good fight and wanted to get compensated for whatever they were going to give me or whatever I agreed to. At that time I would fight just about anybody. That's how it was because my whole life was built around fighting. I just wanted to fight and go to the top. I wanted to make some money. My trainer was a nice person and man, but I look at the stolen opportunities of winning belts and titles as a downfall not just for me but on my trainer's behalf as well. He didn't have the knowledge of the business to dictate or to make a call to dictate fights on my behalf. At least that was how it appeared to me back then. There were some fights I didn't want to take but I took them anyway because of the lack of fights that I was getting. All I could focus on was fighting back then and winning. However, when I did win, the recognition wasn't there. I went into the ring, performed well, and gave the people what they wanted, won the fight, but, still no belt or titles to call my own or to show for it. My trainer didn't understand the business. I was just lucky that I had the skills and a little knowledge that God gave me to use my head because I would be in there with some good guys who were decent fighters. I was really like a Jr. Middleweight, but pulled both classes throughout my whole career. I was fighting full-fledged middleweights. *END OF SESSION 1:*

At least now the fighters get the opportunity to fight. The way some of the business is run why put your fighter in there to fight a guy that is going to be hard. Instead of going through him, if you can fight around him than do that. That is what happened to me. I had contracts signed with guys that went around me and fought for the title and they won. I fought guys and beat champs that had draws with other champs. Things like that happen. Some you win and some you lose. What makes it so easy for them now is that they have many different titles out there. Back then all we had were the World Boxing Organization and World Boxing Council and that was it. It was only two or three belts. Then the IBF came into play. Everybody was in line for those titles. That's all we had back then and we all wanted the opportunity. There were a lot of fighters and everybody wanted the title. You had so many fighters that you had to go through in order to get that opportunity.

PHILLY BOXING HISTORY - Bobby Watts Ring Record

PHILLY BOXING HISTORY							Ring Record - Wat
Home	**Boxers**	**Fights**	**Arenas**	**Non-Boxers**	**Gyms**	**Relics**	**More**	**About**	**Contac**

BOBBY BOOGALOO WATTS
38-7-1 / 20 KO

YEAR	DATE	OPPONENT	RESULT	SITE	VENUE	RELICS
1969	Mar. 13	Teddy Cooper	W6	Baltimore		
	Mar. 28	Alberto Millan	KO4	Baltimore		
	Jun. 30	Carlos Byrd	KO2	Washington, DC		
	Sep. 30	Ron Nesby	W6	Philadelphia	Blue Horizon	POSTER
	Oct. 14	Leroy Roberts	W6	Philadelphia	Blue Horizon	
	Nov. 11	Tommy Shaffer	W6	Philadelphia	Blue Horizon	
1970	Mar. 25	Joe Greene	KO2	Las Vegas		
	Apr. 25	Clarence Geigger	KO'd 6	Las Vegas		
	Sep. 3	Armando Muniz	L6	Los Angeles		
	Nov. 24	Ken Robbins	KO1	Philadelphia	Blue Horizon	
1971	Feb. 9	Roy Edmonds	W6	Philadelphia	Blue Horizon	
	Apr. 29	Perry Abney (Lil' Abner)	KO7	Philadelphia	Arena	
	Jun. 7	Julio Figueroa	W8	Philadelphia	Blue Horizon	
	Aug. 10	Junius Hinton	KO5	Philadelphia	Spectrum	
	Sep. 21	Luis Vinales	W10	Philadelphia	Spectrum	
	Oct. 8	Roy Edmonds	KO5	New York	Felt Forum	POSTER
	Dec. 1	Ralph Palladin	W10	Scranton	Catholic Youth Center	
1972	Apr. 5	Ralph Palladin	D10	Scranton	Catholic Youth Center	
	Jun. 20	Ralph Palladin	KO6	Baltimore		
	Oct. 20	Alvin Phillips	W10	New York	Madison Square Garden	
	Nov. 20	Don Cobbs	KO'd 2	Philadelphia	Spectrum	
1973	Mar. 5	Willie Warren	W10	Philadelphia	Spectrum	
	Apr. 9	Gary Broughton	W10	Philadelphia	Arena	
	May 24	Don Cobbs	KO3	Philadelphia	Arena	
	Jul. 23	Manuel Gonzalez	W10	Philadelphia	Convention Hall	
	Oct. 8	Carlos Alberto Salinas	KO8	Philadelphia	Spectrum	
	Dec. 17	Mario Rosa	W10	New York		
1974	Jul. 15	Cyclone Hart	KO1	Philadelphia	Spectrum	POSTER
	Nov. 12	Willie Monroe	W10	Philadelphia	Spectrum	POSTER, PROGRAM

There were a lot of different fighters with a lot of different styles. I can look at a fighter and see his style and I am more or less able to see and tell him what he needs to take him to another level. There are a lot of fighters that are good up until a certain level after that level they can't go on. The next level is where a fighter wants to get to so that he can experience fights with other outstanding champions and become internationally known. This is where you want to be. You don't just want to be a fighter that comes up, wins the title and just holds the title a couple of times and then you lose it. You want to be the one who wins the title and holds it for a while until you are ready to retire. That is the difference between the types of quality fighter. You don't want to win a title and then the next year you are completely out of it. You want to hold what you earned.

To me boxing was something like the music business. It's like music. You are a star and you want to be in the limelight. You want to continue being that star. You always have to shine and you always want to look good. That's how a fighter is. You have to sell yourself. You have to sell yourself just like an entertainer. Just like the fanciness, the style, the punching or whatever it is that sells you, you have to do something that will attract the eyes of others. Something that you have has to be outstanding to draw the attendance of the crowd.

Buster Drayton had won the IBF championship under my supervision and traineeship. I was okay with the fact that he won the title and I was in his corner all the way. This is something that comes natural for me and I like doing it. It was a pleasure just being there and seeing him win the title under my care. Whatever they say about me or what they think of me helping other athletes getting to a place where they can compete in the sport is fine. That's not really important. It's about being in the atmosphere and in the business. Boxing doesn't make me bitter. I still like the boxing game. I'm still excited about the sport.

Every boxer doesn't come out of the game feeling like this. Everyone has a different attitude towards the boxing sport afterwards. Me, I take it as it comes and just be myself.

I didn't know much about the business, but I knew enough to know that my goal was to go in and fight the guy that was ranked above me so I could move up to the next level. On October 8, 1973 I fought Carlos Salinas from Argentina who had previously fought Benny Briscoe. He dropped Benny, however, Benny came back and stopped him. Carlos was a great puncher too. At the time I fought him he probably had fought over fifty-seven fights. I only had at the most about 25 fights professionally. I thought he had the advantage and the experience because of his long career. I feel like they were testing me to see if I had what it takes. I beat the fight and stopped him in the sixth or seventh round however, it wasn't a walk in the park. It was about a good 4 weeks that I trained for the fight. I was a little jittery about the fight, because this would be my second 10 round fight so I had little experience going in regarding 10 rounders. I wasn't sure what the promoters or the boxing federation ranked me; all I wanted to do was fight the guy who was ahead of me. I thought that was the way it went. That's not how it happened for me, but that is the road that I took at the time. Later, after I hung around and had been in the game a while you learn that you don't have to go through the woodworks to get what you want. You learn that you can maneuver yourself around to get to the title. I was put to the test, by going up against fighters who were preparing to fight for the belt. At this time in my career my managers weren't working for me or doing business for me. They weren't hooking me up with this or that fighter. I wasn't in the drivers seat. I was like a journeyman. I was sort of on the outside looking in. I fought wherever I could fight. Basically for the most of my career, I was the opponent. That is pretty much of what I was. I never had a real promoter. As a manager back then I had a man and woman couple and he didn't know much about boxing, he was just taking whatever was offered to him and I accepted it. They didn't know anything about the game. That is what happened to my career. If I had someone that could talk for me and negotiate contracts and know what goes along with the business it could have been something different. I was just taking whatever they accepted at that time because I wanted to fight. Sometimes I would take fights just to keep the blood in my legs circulating and in good condition. Like in the fight with Carlos Salinas who told me the night of our fight that I wasn't going to run that night.

My two fights in 1974 were with Cyclone Hart and Willie the Worm. The fight with Cyclone Hart was on July 15, 1974. Another Big Showdown. I was always against fighting Cyclone. I never wanted to fight him because we had a close friendship, he had a fierce left hook, he had punching power and he could go the distance and by me not fighting as active as I should have. I was put under a lot of pressure in this fight. I knew I probably wouldn't be able to stand under those guns. The promoters always wanted to put on a good fight. A Jewish promoter in Philadelphia by the name of Russell Peltz ran the tournament in which we fought against each other. I became the aggressor in the fight and won with a one round stoppage by TKO. I had no choice in the matter being that I had no promoter to advocate for me. Other Middleweight fighters like Gil Turner, Charley Scott and Lynn Matthews were fighters before my time. Some of these Middleweight fighters at some point had to go in the rink and jump on one another. I never liked it because I didn't see what the advantage was from doing this. I was always the type of guy that would rather fight a guy from out of state instead of one that is from the same city or state. After you jump on one another, at the end, there's still going to be one left standing and instead of having both continue to compete, one is knocked out of the box.

It didn't happen my way so I did what I had to do.

During that time in 1975 I hadn't fought in a while. When I fought Marshall I think I was laid off for about 10 months prior. I was given about 3 weeks notice for the fight. I sparred about 40 rounds with Matthew Syed Muhammad. I paid him $5.00 per round to get conditioned. I normally sparred anywhere between 100 to 200 rounds before a fight. Prior to Marshall I didn't have any fights at all for a good while. I was just in constant training. I never knew anything about him. I didn't know about his fighting style. I had never seen him fight or looked at him on tape, so I was not familiar with him. I remember people asking as well as this one reporter if I knew anything about Marshall. I would tell them no. And they would say that Marshall was a puncher. He had been all over Europe and knocked out a lot of the Continental champions and different guys that he fought over there. I didn't think anything about him or have anything to say because I didn't know him. I was just presented with a contract to fight him and I was always there to fight. I wanted to fight. They looked at the time I was off and so did I, but I was always ready to fight to make some money so I accepted the fight. I had a plan. My plan was not to get hit. I was prepared physically because of my training and persistence in the gym. I trained quick and hard for him, not knowing his style, I had to be prepared for it. I never had a particular training agenda for a fight; I just trained hard for each fight. I felt that if there were a guy out there that could beat me he would have to have more hands, feet and arms than me. That was my motto. I knew that it would be a hard fight. Right away when I fought him I knew that I couldn't box him because he is a puncher. I couldn't just get in front of him, so I would counter punch him because if I had moved and was off balance I would have been in trouble. James Marshall was awesome and pretty tough. He was the number one Contender. He was getting prepared to fight for the title. I beat him. Before that fight, I only fought twice in 1974.

They were with Cyclone Hart and Willie the Worm. From the late part of 1973 until the end of my career I was practically inactive. I wasn't fighting at all. I was the type of guy that stayed conditioned and if a fight came up and the money was right, I'd be there.

Over the years you forget whom you fought and the years you fought them and where it took place. I think I beat the North Carolina champ also. I do remember going to my hometown where I fought a guy named Willie Ray Taylor for the mid -West title.

Some people ask me what is my particular fighting style. I have been told that I have a style similar to the late great Sugar Ray Robinson. Even all the way to the end of my career, some would say that my style was actually passed down from trainers like Pete Lorenzo, Jack Blackburn and Frank Hamilton. Great fighters such as Joe Louis and Sugar Ray Robinson had a great trainer Jack Blackburn. His trainer and one of the trainers that I had working with me basically passed down a similar fighting style to me.

My boxing style was a mixture of many other fighters' styles with my own unique added twist. I had a combination style where I used Ray Robinson, The Hitman, Thomas Hearns and certain parts of Muhammad Ali's techniques. That was my style. I used my legs, moved around, performed slips and jabs, step-ins and counterpunched.

I can name two great boxers in my opinion of all time. It's tough for me to name my all time favorite boxer. I actually have two. But, basically Sugar Ray Robinson did it all. Also pertaining to Robinson, there were things I could do that Sugar Ray Robinson didn't do. I can practically do anything. Bo Lo punches or upper cuts, double left hooks, I could do all those things. It's just that I didn't have the opportunity to explore myself. My career was cut short. I saw things that Sugar Ray would do that inspired me and I would do them too. For instance, double left hooks and getting around with his hands, taking two steps back and coming in with a punch. Ray Robinson was the one that stands out to me as the worlds greatest.

END OF 2ND SESSION.

Training Days:

Bustle Drayton and I were sparring mates. When I retired he took me in as his trainer in 1987. Every fighter has their own lateral movements so I gave him what he needed to improve his performance as a fighter. While we were training during my career I would tell him things about boxing technique. He saw that what I told him always worked. I was at this level and he chose me to train him. His career was after mine He became a Jr. Middleweight champ – IBF Title in 1987; and did so at a late age. Nonetheless he made it. His record was 17 to 8 when we started. I put him on a winning streak and he only lost one fight before he won the title. I was with Bustle until the fight that he lost to the Canadian boxer. Bustle is still boxing with the youth, comes into the gym from time to time. He definitely has the knowledge and skills to coach.

Another boxer that I trained was Calvin Grove out of Coatesville, PA. In 1989-1990, I was at the casino with Charles Brewer in Atlantic City. Charles was the super middleweight champ at the time. Calvin noticed me and knew the type of fighter that I was, he came over to me and we started talking. We started working together shortly after that. Calvin was a kid that did everything on his own. He was a very independent young man. He didn't come across as having a strong mentor or guardian. He was the type of kid that whatever he had to do he did it. He just had a strong desire to succeed so whatever needed to be done, Calvin met it with great responsibility. After I started working with him and showing him the things that fighters really had to do he took a good liking to me. He knew about the things that I went through and he went through a lot of the same things career wise. The only difference is he made it and I didn't. He did become the IBF featherweight champion, but he wasn't under my wing at the time. At this particular time his mind wasn't settled as to what he wanted to do. He had just come back from Texas where he was training with a lot more Contenders and other champions. He was under the wings of some woman at the time. He left Texas, came back to Philadelphia and was under my wings once again.

Today, I still train guy's part time in the gym while still being employed at the Waterfront where I unload ships, drive tow motors and fork-lifts. I had a lot of guys that used to joke around with me and say "Hey Boogaloo when is your next fight"? Some of them used to joke around with me and say different things about my boxing career. I was retired by then.

My Nightclub Days:

In 1977 I was thinking about moving back to my hometown in South Carolina. I was thinking that if I decided to move back down there I would need a job. I had a little money saved up at this time. I went down there and saw this big nightclub. It was the Riverside Night Club on Highway 76 in East Dover, South Carolina. I met with the guy and gave him so much money up front as an option to buy. I wanted to see how I would do in a years' time. I made sure that I was

locked into the deal so that he would not be able to sell the business until after one year's time. It didn't work out as well as I had expected it to. I was in the business for about 8 months. The whole time I had the nightclub I was still traveling back and forth between South Carolina and Philadelphia. I went into business and didn't know anything about the nightclub business. I was losing money left and right. I lost a lot of money during that time. With every business it's important that you know the business before going in. I was fortunate to have made arrangements with my job at the Waterfront where I had taken a one-year leave of absence. When the nightclub idea didn't work out, before my 1 - year leave of absence was over, I went back to work. I had to go back to work in Philadelphia because I had messed up a lot of money.

My Son's Career:

It would be like starting from scratch. You have to show your ability and that you are capable of being great in the boxing sport.

If you take this approach, you would have to build a reputation and sell yourself to the public even more.

It's easier to sell yourself if you win the Gold medal or a medal from the Olympics because you are already internationally well known due to all of the exposure. If you come out from the armed service, you may be well known in a couple of states so you have to push harder for recognition.

During the times I was boxing I still had to work at the waterfront between fights. I had to work because I couldn't live off of what I was making from boxing alone. After each of my major fights my job would give me a week before and after the fight so I would pack up and go down south and see my people. In between fights I used to take trips and go down south a lot. This is why I like big cars. They grip the road when you're driving. I remember I had a Lincoln Coupe with a white top and gangster white walls. A lot of kids used to come up to me and say, "Hey Mister, are you a pimp?" I used to have spokes in my wheels and I used to get stopped by the cops about three times a day. They would ask me "Where you working at?" That was one of the reasons why I put my name on the back of my car, because I used to get stopped all the time. When I put my name on my car, some of the police would drive up on me and read my name and then they would back off. When I put my name on the back of my trunk, it helped. When people would see Bobby Boogaloo Watts with a pair of boxing gloves on the rear of the driver's side, they would blow their horns. My favorite car was a 1976 black Lincoln with all white interior. It had a long front and a short back with white wheels. I remember you used to have some kind of insert that you would put in the wheel to further pimp out the ride. I had a gangster lean but wasn't a gangster. I had a pimped out ride, but wasn't a pimp. Nothing is changed today, when the cops see a young man driving in a nice car they are quick to pull you over and ask for your license. I remember once when I was pulled over the officer asked me to show him my license. I would get out of the car and then once I was out of the car and standing, they used to look up and say, "Oh I didn't realize that you were that tall." It was something how the cars back then had a lot of legroom. I have long legs and a short trunk so that made me look short. So I use to get out of the car and then they would recognize me and let me drive off.

Once there was a write up about how hard I worked at my job and in the boxing game. I had purchased a nice 2 story, 4 bedroom house, a big sound soul Cadillac parked in front of my 4 bedroom, 2 story house that I purchased. I always worked hard and I was able to gain and enjoy the fruits of my labor. I had to work a steady job to pay my bills and to live like this. Today guys who fight have more of an opportunity to live off of the money they make from 1 fight. They have more opportunity to invest and manage their money. They invest in clubs and other businesses, which brings them more money. *END OF SESSION III.*

his way, but Eubank squeezed by on points in Glasgow, Scotland. One year later he lost on points Tulsa, OK, to Jame Toney in a fight Thornton simply did not do enough to win. He mounted one last drive in 1995, winning the USBA title at 168 with a second-round blowout of Darren Zenner at the Blue Horizon and that netted him his biggest payday when h was stopped in three rounds later that year in Pensacola, FL, by Roy Jones. A popular fighter with a big following, Thornton did not lose until his 19th fight when Doug DeWitt beat him in a 13th-round boxoff for the USBA middleweight title. He was 9-0 from 1990 through mid-1992 with wins ove Dave Tiberi, Karama Leota and Merqui Sosa. His record was 37-7-1, 26 Kos.

Who...Bobby "Boogaloo" Watts
From...North Philadelphia
The Facts...The best boxer of the three young Philadelphia middleweights of the 1970s--Eugene "Cyclone" Hart and Willie "The Worm" Monroe were the other two--Watts was the first man to beat Marvin Hagler when he gained a 10-round majority decision in 1976 at The Spectrum. Watts turned pro in 1969 but his career stalled by the end of the yea and he traveled to the West Coast where two losses in three fights sent him home. He resumed his career and beat good fighters like Roy Edmonds, Li'l Abner, Ralph Palladin, Willie Warren and Mario Rosa. He defeated Hart and Monroe in 1974 at The Spectrum, but never capitalized, even after beating Hagler. A knockout loss in 1977 to David Love in San Antonio, TX, ruined his title hopes and ended his 13-fight winning streak. One year later, Mustafa Hamsho Kod him in Jersey City, NJ, and his days as a contender were over. Hagle got revenge in 1980 and, after four wins, Watts retired in 198 after getting Kod by Mark Kaylor in London. His record was 38-7-1, 20 Kos.

Who...Prince Charles Williams
From...Mansfield, OH
The Facts...Light-heavyweight Prince Charles Williams was discovered while losing a 10-round decision to former two-time world champion Marvin Johnson on an ESPN-televised show in 1984 in Indianapolis. J Russell Peltz, who promoted Johnson, was impressed with Williams' desire and he signed the Mansfield, OH, prospect. Peltz brought in veteran Marty

Boxing has been a part of my life since I was 14 years old. I like the game and love to participate in it. The longest stint I did away from boxing is 2 months. I've been to a lot of the big gyms around the country and developed friendships and connections for over 40 years. Boxing to me is like any other type of sport. It can take you around the world. It has taken me across ¾ of the world. You learn a lot from the sport. Your quality of sportsmanship can take you around the world if you have the ability.

I trained Roger Matagua a pure African who is a young professional world-class fighter. He is a good listener, a good fighter who was willing to try different things. He wasn't limited in his thoughts. He seemed to have made a transformation under my direction. Roger fought in Chicago, Illinois on November 10, 2006. He did a tremendous job during the fight that lasted for 12 rounds. Based on the opinion of the referees he came up a little short. Even though he lost the fight, he looked good losing. A lot of people including myself felt that he won that fight. After the fight, they had to rush the other fighter to the hospital to get stitched up. Roger came in and went out looking the same way. He still has a lot left in him. He's only about 27 years old. He still has time. He has some years left in him providing he doesn't take a lot of punishment. If he doesn't take punishment he can go until he's older. A small fighter doesn't last as long as a bigger fighter. A heavyweight can go until they are about 38 to 40 years. A middleweight fighter can go until they are 30 to 35 years. The middleweight is the hardest class in the division. They come in all shapes and sizes. They come tall, short, medium, and range from soft to hard hitters. When we arrived at the arena for the fight, it was like we stepped into a Mexican neighborhood. The kid he fought was Mexican.

His producer is Mexican. Golden Boy Productions, De La Hoya is his promoter and he does his own thing now. His fight was produced and managed by Oscar De La Hoya. When I walked into the auditorium, I thought I was in Mexico. The Mexicans must have traveled from all over to see this fight. The whole place was jam-packed. I like how the Mexicans show up to support their hometown hero. When you fight in an opponent's backyard sometimes you feel like you are in their kitchen or living room and put on the spot to perform. This is sort of what happened that night. This was an elimination bout so the winner will go on to fight for the IBF championship. Roger won't drop down too far in rank. He'll be back. If he fights two more times he'll be ready for another shot. When you go into another fighter's back yard you need to give them a little extra and you have to beat them a little more. Sometimes you have to do a little extra. Television viewers watched the fight and said that Roger should have won the fight. Quite a few people came up to me and stated that Roger did a tremendous job and he looked much different than the time when he was training under someone else. His manager was very pleased with my type of training and it was just that Roger came up a little short this time. I am confident the next time around he'll do better.

Boxing has always been a part of me and whatever I can handle and take on I'm going to try it. If you have just one trainer and you have a thousand fighters there is not enough trainers with fighters so you have to take on as much as you can handle. Training has been a big part of my career and life and I hope to continue to give to the sport and train as the fighters come along. Some people come along and want to participate in training for the sport at times, but they have to be dedicated. It's not what you do when you are in the gym, it's what you do when you leave there. You have to be dedicated when you are trying to make a career of boxing or any other field. You have to put the time in. If you are good to it, it will be good to you.

Sometimes when I'm training a guy, I might have other guys as well. My other fighters are kind of put to the side for a moment as the more advanced fighter prepares for his upcoming fight. I had to explain that I wasn't overlooking them or anything like that. If they were in that position, I would do the same for them. You have to get the work when and wherever you can get it. Each fighter has to want to be in the ring. It is up to them. If the guys show up to the gym, I can teach them what I know and I am willing to take them as far as I can go. If they don't show up and they don't want it, there's nothing that I can do for them. Roger wanted it, he was a good listener and he tried different things. When you do that you make it easier for yourself when you listen. There's a lot of fighters that get in there just because they had a couple of fights and get these belts and they think they know everything but they can easily be beaten. In Roger's case, he lost the fight but he looked good losing. He didn't take any punishment. He reminds me of a biblical fighter. Some fighters do as their trainer tells them and some fighters compliment this by adding their own technique to what they are taught. This is what Roger did. This will help a fighter prepare to do a little more and then they are able to stand on their own two feet in the ring. I say this because your trainer may not be able to attend each and every fight with the boxer he trained. So therefore, the fighter might have to go in the ring without his trainer present. He still has to perform. For instance, in the Olympics, your main trainer is not there. You are taking instruction from the coaches. That's why it's important to be broken in correctly so that the confidence is there within to perform. The bottom line is that it is up to the fighter. It is what he wants not the trainer. If he wants to win, then he will put his best effort toward the fight. You have to be capable of standing where you are, or you will be the type of fighter that stands on the outside

looking in. The gym has to be a fighters' first priority. You have to make that number one. This has to be the key. This is the only way you are going to make it. You can't put the gym second or third, it has to be number one.

I noticed that a lot of kids come into the gym and say that they want to be a fighter. It is the only thing they dreamed of doing. Sometimes, it only takes one shot. I have seen fighters that come in to the gym and train for months. As soon as they get in the ring and get hit one time pretty decent, this will be the most prominent determining factor if they really want to box. If they come back they want it. Some never come back after getting beat up or dropped. I have been socked, dropped and I have been hit so hard that I staggered in the ring. That didn't stop me because I wanted it. I wouldn't allow myself to be

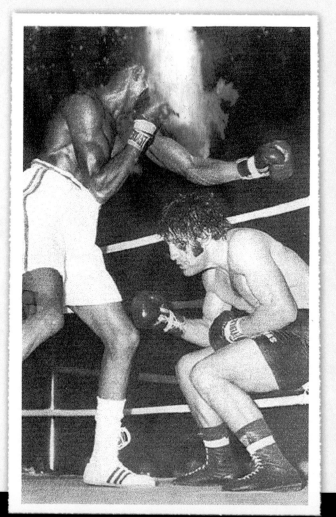

overpowered.   So I got up, brushed my pants off and continued on. That's how it is in boxing and in life in general.

The ones that take the bitter with the sweet and learn how to bounce back are the ones that really want it.

When I was younger it seems like I didn't get the recognition as I do today. Even the little children see me and yell out "Hey Mr. Boogaloo". That strikes me funny because when I look at them I know that they weren't around to see me fight or to do the "Boogaloo". I ride the train up to Cecil B. Moore and as I walk to the gym, the kids are sitting around when I come up and they speak as if they know me. I believe they have heard of me through their parents and from those during my generation as well as my exposure in the neighborhood and their access to me via the gym. Some guys still come up to me and ask me if I remember them from 23rd Street, which has been torn down for a good while now.   These are grown men with children now and they say they are going to bring their sons down to see me in the gym.   I have seen the generations change.

I am not looking to stand out, be fabulous or to be spectacular or in the limelight. I am simply doing what I love to do and I do it well. My gift from God is the strength to do what I do pertaining to training and the boxing industry.

The "Boogaloo" was the name of a dance. In Vineland, New Jersey, I was fighting for the championship against Johnny Jones – The Shingaling. I would come

out doing the "Boogaloo". That's how I got my name and I wear it proudly.

A Champion without a Crown is the title of my book. I chose this name because it reflects my career. After my boxing career came to an end, I am here today training kids in boxing. Some don't have the skills or lack the ability that I had and they still have more opportunity.   I always felt that I was a champion back then and still do today, however, I also feel that I was robbed of a lot of opportunity.

I dedicate this book to my entire family who scream of Bobby Watts blood in their veins.   I also would like to thank my fans. I hope they like my book and will continue to support my efforts in life and in the boxing industry.

END OF SESSION IV:

Watts wants fight with Briscoe as step toward middleweight title

By Gene Courtney
Inquirer Staff Writer

Bobby Watts' patience is wearing a little bit thin. The tall, lanky boxer from North Philadelphia has established himself as the best, young middleweight prospect in the city through a series of elimination bouts in which he beat Willie Monroe in 10 rounds and knocked out Eugene (Cyclone) Hart in one.

But despite that, Watts feels that he hasn't made very much progress since he started boxing professionally in March, 1969, and he's very disturbed that Monroe — a man he defeated — is ranked one notch above him at No. 6 in the Ring Magazine ratings.

He has compiled a record of 29 victories, three losses and one draw and he has not lost since November, 1972, when he was knocked out by Don Cobb of St. Louis in the second round — his only knockout defeat.

Watts has won 11 bouts in a row and he is hoping to chalk up No. 12 when he meets Casey Gacic (13-3-3) in the feature 10-round bout tomorrow night at Convention Hall. Gacic from Cleveland is a substitute for Lenny Harden of New York, who pulled out of the fight because of an injury to his right hand in training.

And that is another of the minor irritants with which Watts must cope.

"I've had so many signed contracts with so many guys," Watts said, "like Lloyd Nelson, Ike White, (the late) Leroy Roberts and others and I train and then the fights don't come off."

The result is that Watts has been averaging a little over four bouts a year and the periods of inactivity are particularly vexing to him. He feels that is the main reason why his progress toward a title bout — the dream of every boxer — has been impeded.

The baby-faced six-footer is still grubbing for purses a lot smaller than he thinks he should earn and for the opportunity to work regularly at bashing in other people's faces.

"The only way I'll ever get anywhere," said the 26-year-old boxer-puncher, "is to fight the guys who are rated above me. I feel if a man has a high rating he should stand behind it and fight anybody and the guy I'd like to fight now is Bennie Briscoe (rated No. 4 by Ring Magazine)."

And that is another departure from Watts' previous philosophy of refusing to fight local boxers because he saw no sense "in knocking each other off."

"We certainly want to fight Briscoe," said Mrs. Sylvia Booker, his manager, "but we can't find a promoter to put the fight on. I think that Bobby and Bennie could be the best possible fight that could be made as far as making money is concerned.

"Peltz (Spectrum promoter J. Russell) wants us to fight Monroe again but what will that prove? We've already beaten Monroe."

Watts agreed: "We don't need Monroe. If it comes down to getting closer to a championship fight, I'll fight anybody who can move me up to it."

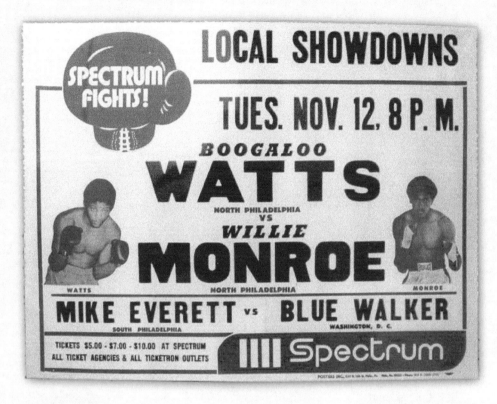

LOCAL SHOWDOWNS

SPECTRUM FIGHTS!

TUES. NOV. 12, 8 P. M.

BOOGALOO
WATTS
NORTH PHILADELPHIA
VS
WILLIE
MONROE
NORTH PHILADELPHIA

WATTS

MONROE

MIKE EVERETT VS BLUE WALKER
SOUTH PHILADELPHIA

WASHINGTON, D. C.

TICKETS $5.00 - $7.00 - $10.00 AT SPECTRUM
ALL TICKET AGENCIES & ALL TICKETRON OUTLETS

||||| Spectrum

POSTERS INC., 547 N. 10th St. Phila. Pa.

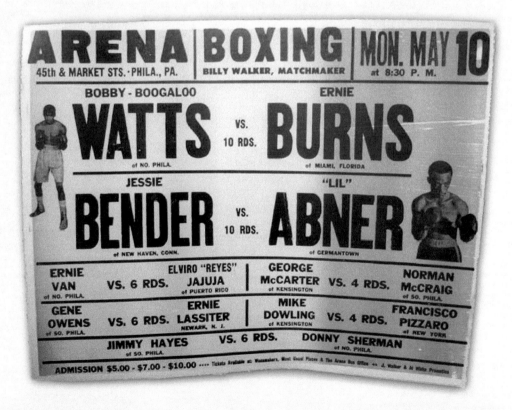

ARENA | BOXING | MON. MAY 10
45th & MARKET STS. · PHILA., PA. | BILLY WALKER, MATCHMAKER | at 8:30 P. M.

BOBBY - BOOGALOO   ERNIE
WATTS VS. BURNS
 of NO. PHILA.   10 RDS.   of MIAMI, FLORIDA

JESSIE   "LIL"
BENDER VS. ABNER
of NEW HAVEN, CONN.   10 RDS.   of GERMANTOWN

ERNIE VAN of NO. PHILA.	VS. 6 RDS.	ELVIRO "REYES" JAJUJA of PUERTO RICO	GEORGE McCARTER of KENSINGTON	VS. 4 RDS.	NORMAN McCRAIG of SO. PHILA.
GENE OWENS of SO. PHILA.	VS. 6 RDS.	ERNIE LASSITER NEWARK, N. J.	MIKE DOWLING of KENSINGTON	VS. 4 RDS.	FRANCISCO PIZZARO of NEW YORK

JIMMY HAYES VS. 6 RDS. DONNY SHERMAN
of SO. PHILA.   of NO. PHILA.

ADMISSION $5.00 - $7.00 - $10.00 .... Tickets Available at Wanamakers, Most Local Places & The Arena Box Office .... J. Walker & Al White Presents

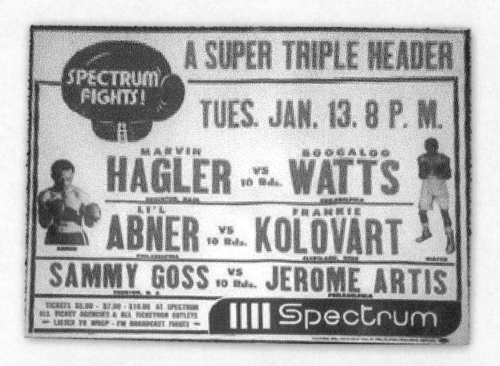

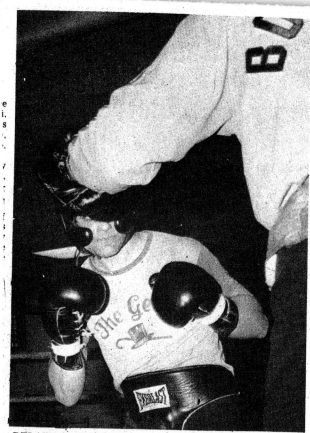

DELAWARE COUNTY'S George Plimpton peers at Bobby "Boogaloo" Watts while regretting each and every Big Mac and French fry he had consumed for the past year. Somehow, they stayed in Pete's stomach and he survived to write this article, which does not include a demand for a rematch.

(Ethan Prescott Photo)

The SPORTING Life

PETE INNAURATO

NEWS Writer No Paper Tiger With Boogaloo

George Plimpton, the gutsy writer who has dedicated his journalistic career to doing weird things, has suddenly become my idol.

You remember good ol' George, don't you? Played quarterback for the Detroit Lions during an exhibition game. Pitched to an all-star lineup at Yankee Stadium. Sparred Archie Moore three rounds until the ex-light heavy king bloodied George's mush . . .

CRAZY GEORGE WROTE about all his adventures. Some people said he was wifty. Others said he was immature.

But good ol' George showed them. He laughed all the way to PSFS and back.

Yep, crazy George Plimpton is full of zany angles. That's why I borrowed a chapter out of his unpredictable career last Friday.

I have no idea whatsoever as to how my getting in the ring with Bobby "Boogaloo" Watts, the best middleweight in Philadelphia, came about. Someone suggested it would be a good angle for the paper. Others said it would be a good way to get amnesia.

But I decided to lace the 16-ouncers up. After all, I figure would be fighting in front of over 300 people who showed up the second annual Big Brothers "Show of Champions." A thing like this is good publicity.

"NOW, DON'T YOU try taking Boogaloo out with one of your

shots," Tony Beltrante, an ex-featherweight who worked my corner, warned me.

"Thanks for the advice," I said. "You really know how to boost my ego."

I had trained hard for this brawl. Potato chips and beer. Gino Giants and milkshakes. Lasagna and wine. Never felt worse in my life.

For two minutes I was throwing bombs. Uppercuts. Hooks. Jabs. Crosses. I would occasionally do the Ali shuffle and deliver 30 straight bolo punches.

Ah, round one was ready to begin. . .

BOOGALOO WATTS came out of his corner and contemplated my style. He looked like he had never seen anything like it. But that was my strategy. I wanted to puzzle him.

Snap! His left jab had met up with my Adams apple. I got this sudden urge to pray.

"You're doing fine," Tony Beltrante yelled. "Press him. Press him."

All I wanted to do was pay Boogaloo off. Maybe a ten spot would make him take a fall.

Ding!

I HEADED BACK to my corner as the bell ended round one. I was satisfied to have lasted three whole minutes with a world class boxer.

"Keep your hands up," Tony Beltrante instructed me. "Stay on top of him. Punch to his body."

"Right," I said. "But slip me a pipe just in case."

Tony laughed. He thought I was joking. But man, I don't joke about such things.

Boogaloo Watts stormed out of his corner for round two. Immediately he employed a machine-gun jab that had me wishing I had never heard of George Plimpton and his catalog of nutty schemes.

I STALKED BOOGALOO, desperately trying to connect with one of my famous cockeyed left hooks.

Wham! I reached back and let go with a punch that would have knocked down a fight arena. George Plimpton would have been proud.

Unfortunately, Boogaloo Watts was not the recipient of the lethal weapon. He stood in the opposite end of the ring watching me left hook air to death.

The bell rang ending the fiasco. I vowed I would never condemn crazy George Plimpton again.

"MAN, YOU CAN fight," Boogaloo Watts told me after our fistic affair. "You're strong. Real strong."

I told Boogaloo I was appreciative of the compliment. After all, one should be proud to have lasted a couple rounds with a guy who is listed among the 10 top middleweights in the world.

"You did good," Joey O'Donnell, who coordinated the show, said. "Covered up nice."

"Thanks," I said. "But next time you want someone to spar Boogaloo Watts, call George Plimpton."

Phantomweights in Rare Philly Feature

By GARY SMITH

Thirty-nine years ago they let a couple of 118-pound squirts climb into the ring for the main event at Shibe Park.

There was no choice that night. You can't very well stash a world title fight in the middle of your four-round preliminaries.

It never happened again in Philadelphia. Except for a few dingy club fights here and there, no promoter has dared play the trumpets and roll the drums for guys whose ribs show.

Until tonight. Jeff Chandler of South Philadelphia and Javier Flores of Salt Lake City meet in the 12-round main event of this evening's 8 o'clock Spectrum card, the first time bantamweights have received such a pedestal in this city since the 1941 Tom Forte-Lou Salica championship bout.

THE AMERICAN sports fan pays to see 118-pound men only if they're riding in the fifth at Keystone. Why go to the Spectrum and pay to see two elves blow bubbles at each other for 12 rounds?

That is the mentality which promoter Russell Peltz head-butts against in tonight's card.

"This is a major fight but it may go unappreciated because of the American fans' mentality that only the bigger fighters are interesting," fretted Peltz. "If this fight was in Mexico, you couldn't get in the place. It's tough for Americans, who are basi-

Photographed by Sam Psoras

Bobby (Boogaloo) Watts and Jeff Chandler at weigh-in

cally not that small, to get excited about little guys.

"People like to imagine themselves being in the ring. It's tough to do that with 118-pounders. It's tough to identify with them. In Mexico you can shake a tree and 25 bantamweights fall out, so they associate with them better.

"I think Jeff Chandler has the potential to be a world champion. And if he's good enough to be a champion, he certainly qualifies to fight in a main event in his hometown."

Jeff Chandler would have been main-event material a year ago if he'd asked for second helpings as a kid. He is 19-0-1 with eight knockouts and is rated by many as the best East Coast bantamweight in the last quarter century.

He owns the USBA title and a win against the talented Flores (26-4-3) tonight would give him the North American Boxing Federation crown and a top 10 WBC rating. A top 10 ABC rating, too. If Chandler beats his toughest opponent to date and gets a title shot, that network would no doubt grab for it.

"THEY'RE TIRED of showing two Spanish guys fighting (in the lighter weights) for the title," explained Peltz.

The possibilities excite Chandler and and his handlers and his close relatives and nobody else. The kid's weight classification is all wrong. He should be listed as a phantomweight.

He is a gnat that wandered into a beehive by mistake. In this city a fighter had better spike his punch with the strong stuff. Give 'em Curtis Parker and some skull to whomp on any old time. The hell with two little men flitting in and out, in and out with scientific precision and artistic flourish.

"Big guys make a sluggish fight," argued the 23-year-old boxer. "Nobody wants to come to fights and fall asleep. I guarantee that won't happen. This will be two little guys banging at a much quicker pace.

"I thought I shoulda been in the main event a while back. The promoters didn't. They'll catch on."

Jeff Chandler and Curtis Parker are Philadelphia's two potential champions. Parker's style is a throat-grabber, Chandler's is a batted eyelash. It has been difficult for Chandler to sit back and watch Parker grab all the throats and all the publicity.

"Look at Curtis Parker," said Chandler. "I've had more fights and I'm still undefeated. I'm rated as high and he gets more publicity. It's hard to take this all in. I'm just as good or

better. My boxing outweighs his slugging. It makes me wonder.

"THEY SAY I can't punch. I have seven knockouts in my last 11 fights. I don't know what you call this. I'm not a one-punch knockout fighter but the way I throw them in volleys can put a man down. I'm what fights are all about.

"But I go to amateur and pro fights around town and a lotta guys don't even know who I am. You introduce yourself and then you see them tug an arm of someone else and say, 'Who is that guy?'"

Chandler realized just how bad things had gotten last summer, when he was scheduled for the main event at Steel Pier. Fight day drew near and still there were no posters advertising it. Finally Chandler demanded some from the promoter and went around Philadelphia posting them himself.

"You know you're hurting when you gotta do it yourself," he said. "I like to go out and meet the people — that's my style — but I don't think I should have to do that. If I didn't walk up to you and tell you about that fight, you wouldn't have known it was coming off. And the posters were only the size of loose-leaf paper."

Tonight the 118-pound man finally gets his chance to grow. He is learning his lesson the hard way. Plastering someone else's face is much better advertisement than plastering your own poster.

Injury may stall Hagler

Middleweight champion Marvin Hagler was examined by his personal physician, Dr. Nishan Keckejian, in Brockton last night, and will undergo further testing in the form of a bone scan this morning at Cardinal Cushing Hospital in Brockton.

Hagler, in training for a scheduled July 15 defense against Venezuelan Fulgencio Obelmejiac in San Remo, Italy, injured his ribs on Tuesday night while sparring with Bobby "Boogaloo" Watts. No determination on when Hagler may resume training will be made until after today's examination.

Hagler was taken to the Cape Cod Hospital in Hyannis Tuesday night where he was examined for over two hours and a chest x-ray was taken, determining that he had not suffered a broken bone.

"He came in on his own steam and was never admitted to the hospital so it was not too serious," said a hospital spokesman. "I don't think the doctors gave him a timetable but they certainly told him to take it easy until the soreness goes away."

— GEORGE KIMBALL

stretched over a "I've stayed in boxing because I weight title even though the late'

Hagler KO Evens Count on Watts

By THOM GREER

PORTLAND, Me. — If Bobby (Boogaloo) Watts and Marvin Hagler are permitted to battle for a third time inside the round circle it's likely the judges will be selected from the ranks of the FBI and the timekeeper will be named by Pope John Paul II. And even then, the outcome would probably ignite a controversy that the United Nations General Assembly would be hard-pressed to resolve.

Watts-Hagler fights spark more protracted public dispute than Russian invasions of underdeveloped nations.

Watts' questionable decision over Hagler in their first meeting was called "highway robbery" by most fans in the Spectrum that night in January 1976. And the Pennsylvania State Athletic Commission must have agreed because the judges in that fight, Earl Vann and Nate Lopinson, have never worked another fight.

HAGLER AVENGED that defeat at the Civic Center here yesterday by gaining a knockout, according to timekeeper Francis Anderson, at 3:09 of the second round. Try that one on for size, Mr. Ripley.

Well, the official record was revised to show Watts lost by a knockout at 2:59. But by Anderson's clock, as well as the clock maintained by the ABC television crew, the time was 3:09.

The difficulty arose because Anderson, a taxi driver by profession, did not know that the rules of the Maine State Athletic Commission permit a fighter to be saved by the bell. Even if he is flat on his back his trainers can drag him to the corner and try to revive him for the next round.

When Hagler unleashed a crushing right hook that floored Watts for the second time with only three seconds left in the round, Anderson stopped the clock as Referee Rene LaLiberte began his count. Anderson started the clock again when Watts pulled himself upright at the count of nine.

Anderson started the clock. As Watts struggled to right himself, the bell sounded a split second before the fighter slipped back down to

Referee motions Marvin Hagler to neutral corner after Hagler dropped Bobby (Boogaloo) Watts in first round

"I never said I wanted to quit (as LaLiberte   ready for a Marvin Hagler in five days. And he   victory. "No way. We (fighters in the ring)

Money Dispute Cancels Hearns-Watts Bout

United Press International

DETROIT — Today's scheduled middleweight fight between Thomas Hearns and Bobby "Boogaloo" Watts was cancelled last night over a money dispute between promoter Joe Wright and Hearns' manager, Emanuel Steward.

Steward said he pulled Hearns and five other boxers from the fight when a local attorney making his debut as a boxing promoter indicated he would not be able to pay the fighters.

"He had been trying to get the fight televised and had planned on using that money to pay the fighters," Steward said. "But the television plans fell through and he said he had no other money."

Jeffrey May of Escot Boxing, the coordinator of the event, said Wright failed to post a $125,000 letter of credit due Sept. 17 to cover half of Hearns'

$250,000 purse.

Watts was to be paid $50,000. The entire program apparently required gross receipts of $350,000 before Wright and his sponsors could break even.

Ticket sales had been slow for the fight, which was set for the Joe Louis Arena. May said they had sold only $50,000 worth of tickets for the match. A spokesman at the arena said tickets ranging n price from $10 to $40 would be refunded.

Wright insisted "a very minor problem" was behind the cancellation.

"I don't want to get into the details," Wright said. "But we paid all the bills we were obligated to pay up to this time," the attorney said. "The fighters had been taken care of.

"At one time — three or four days ago — we were extremely close to selling   In fact, I had

been led to believe we had it, until all that changed a day ago.

"To some degree, I think people were taking advantage of my naivete," Wright said.

This is the second cancellation of a Hearns fight in four months. Hearns' scheduled middleweight championship bout with with Marvin Hagler in May was postponed by a hand injury to Hearns, then cancelled when negotiations to re-schedule it fell through.

World Boxing Council, has given Sugar Ray Leonard until the end of November to decide whether he will continue boxing or give up his world welterweight title.

Leonard regained the World Boxing Council title in November, 1980, when Roberto Duran quit in the eighth round of their championship bout in New Orleans. He added the World Boxing Association version in

September, 1981, stopping Hearns in 14 rounds.

Leonard, who has earned over $40 million in boxing, said he would make a decision on his future in the ring sometime next month. He has indicated that he is leaning toward retirement rather than risking the sight in his surgically-repaired eye.

Roberto Duran, the former world lightweight and welterweight champion, said last night he had no plans to retire, despite a recent upset loss to unknown Kirkland Laing on Sept. 4 in Detroit.

The 31-year-old Duran said he had signed a promotional contract with Bob Arum's Top Rank, Inc., and that he will be fighting on the undercard of the Aaron Pryor-Alexis Arguello World Boxing   welterweight

Thomas Hearns: no money

Boogaloo longing for the big bucks

By BOB WRIGHT
Of The Bulletin Staff

Bobby (Boogaloo) Watts, who is scheduled to make an infrequent public appearance later this week, admits things have not gone well since he won the J. Russell Peltz Gets Tough boxing tournament.

Peltz, who will promote Watts' scheduled 10-round bout with Cincinnati's Clifford Wills in the 69th st. Forum Tuesday, told local managers in 1974 that the Spectrum might get out of the fight business unless they stopped refusing matches between ranked Philadelphians.

Faced with the prospect of underemployment, the managers allowed the promoter to throw Bennie Briscoe, Cyclone Hart, Willie Monroe, Watts and outsider Emile Griffith into his Spectrum meatgrinder.

Watts finished the nine-month orgy on his feet, claimed the middleweight championship of Philadelphia and announced that he would "like to retire at 30 and be middleweight champion of the world."

Boogaloo will turn 30 on Nov. 11.

"It doesn't look like I'll be retired," Watts said the other day. "I'd still like to be champion, but only for the money. I work steady (on a loading dock); we're not hungry. I've got a nice family (wife, Judy; three daughters). Things are okay. The title has never been somethin' I had to have, but I would like some of that big money."

Peltz wishes Boogaloo had been hungry when he was younger.

"He could have been dynamite," the promoter said, wistfully. "I always thought it came apart in '72. He was fighting Don Cobbs on a Deborah show at the Spectrum. Watts came out showboating like he really could. The crowd was eating it up when Cobbs caught him with a looping right hand. Bobby got up but he didn't quite beat the count. After that it seemed like he was always too cautious, never willing to take a chance. He got dull."

Watts won eight mostly dull fights over the next two years, getting even with Cobbs in one of them, then began to disappear more regularly than a magician's assistant. He's fought nine times in the past 57 months; hasn't fought at home since 1976.

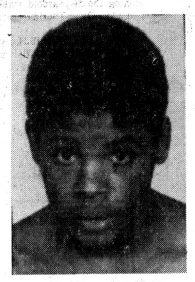

Bobby (Boogaloo) Watts

"He started asking big money for not-so-big opponents," said Peltz.

"I'm in this for the money," said Watts. "They don't want to pay, I don't have to fight. I had other problems, too, though. For one thing, I get a lot of colds. My doctor says it's from workin' outside. I get bundled up, then I start sweatin' so I take off some stuff. I catch a cold, I get a virus. Sometimes I've had to pull out (of fights) because of that."

Watts (32-6-1, 14 KOs) will be making his first appearance this year against Wills, who is 31 and owns a 14-7-1 log that includes four knockouts.

The Sunday Bulletin   March 19, 1978

Watts Eager to Get Going

"My goal? I would like to retire at 30 and be the middleweight champion on the world."

—Bobby (Boogaloo) Watts, Oct. 1974.

By LEROY SAMUELS
Of The Bulletin Staff

Next Monday, the 27th, fighter Bobby (Boogaloo) Watts will have an anniversary he would like to forget. He will be inactive for an entire year.

Bobby Watts is 28, has a 29-4-1 record, goes to Joe Frazier's gymnasium on North Broad five days a week, is in physical shape, has a new manager in Bob Brown, is advised by his cousin, heavyweight Jimmy Young, and last month turned down a 10-round fight with Willie (The Worm) Monroe at the Spectrum.

"I didn't want that fight," said Watts, "because I'm not a middleweight anymore. I'm a junior middleweight."

There doesn't appear to be an enormous demand for junior middleweights, who have a 154-pound limit (middleweights have a 160 limit), but Watts is convinced "I can get a quicker chance at a world title this way."

Watts said this upstairs, in a corridor at Frazier's gymnasium. He sat on a folding chair, his gym bag at this side. "I've been fighting light against middleweights all my life," said Watts. "I've been the guy giving away pounds for years. Now, I'm going to fight guys my own weight."

Four years ago, Bobby Watts used to boast how he cleaned this city of its middleweights. J. Russell Peltz, the Spectrum boxing director, had a

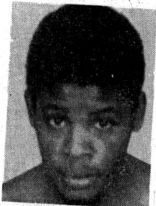

Bobby (Boogaloo) Watts

middleweight tournament and Watts beat up Monroe to open the series. Then, Emile Griffith of New York City upset Bennie Briscoe. Watts then knocked out Eugene (Cyclone) Hart.

But Bobby Watts was never very active following those stunning victories. "When we wanted to use Bobby Watts, we just couldn't get his name on a contract. There were lots of reasons given," complained Peltz.

Watts said his former manager, Mrs. Sylvia Booker, was a "beautiful lady who treated me all right but I just couldn't get enough fights with her. And, I really do like to keep busy."

The last fight which was signed was a disaster. Watts fought David Love nearly a year ago. In the second round, Love knocked down Watts. In the fourth, Love knocked him down

again and the fight was stopped. Watts hasn't fought since then.

Brown said several opponents are presently being considered for Watts.

"We're not going to rush and grab the first junior middleweight who is available," said Brown. "We're going to take our time and look for the right fighter."

Watts said he has the patience to wait again. "But I'm not getting any younger," he said.

● ● ●

Frank Gelb, who is the co-manager of light-heavyweight Matt Franklin, said he and J. Russell Peltz are not "seeing eye-to-eye on what I think

Again After Year Layoff

Matthew is worth for a Spectrum main event." Gelb: "Russell and I are friends, but I have to look out for my fighter. The life of a fighter is so short and it is my obligation to see he gets the money he deserves. Right now, Russell and I are apart on money figures."...That was one reason Peltz could not announce a Matt Franklin vs. Willie Taylor fight for April. "Russell called me from ringside on Tuesday and asked if he could announce the fight and I said no, let's wait."

So, Peltz will have a co-feature on April 10. Smoking Wade Hinnant will fight junior lightweight Ricardo Ar-

rendondo (61-14-1, 44 KOs) and Skinny Jimmy Rothwell will meet a welterweight to be named. Peltz: "I think Hinnant is better than Howard Davis and Rothwell is better than Sugar Ray Leonard. It's just the other two have had more television exposure."

Augie Pantellas needed four stitches below the left eye after scoring 10-round decision over Rom. Contreras on Tuesday. Pantellas' handlers are suggesting a rematch, possibly for May. "Maybe that will convince the newspaper people who really won the fight the last time," said Marty Feldman, who manages Pantellas....The Mike Everett-

Bruce Curry fight fell through...Richie Kates, battered by Franklin last month, will probably fight a tuneup in Atlantic City in June or July...Willie (The Worm) Monroe, inactive since a TKO loss to Marvin Haigler last August, may fight next month.

Watts TKOs Cincinnatian

By BOB WRIGHT
Of The Bulletin Staff

Onetime contender Bobby (Boogaloo) Watts last night kicked off what he hopes will be his last comeback and first real run at a boxing championship.

Watts, two weeks away from his 30th birthday, ended an 11-month layoff at Upper Darby's 69th st. Forum, collecting a technical knockout when Clifford Wills quit 10 seconds into the third round.

Wills, a 31-year-old Cincinnati boxer who showed the effects of having gone the distance in losses to several ranked fighters, said he quit because of impared vision.

"The (right) eye was puffin' up, from that really good shot he (Watts) hit me in the first round," said Wills. "When the guy put the ice pack on it, between the second and third, he jammed it too hard. It felt like the edge of the ice cube hit my eyeball. When I went to get up, I was seein' double."

It was obvious from the outset that the head-taller Watts was too quick and too clever for Wills (14-8-1). The North Philadelphian scored with several quick combinations. One including a right to the body followed by a left hook to the eye and it established his superiority midway through the opening round.

"I been inactive, but I guess I still got it," said Watts. "Timing is still a little off, but the hands felt quick. Now I feel like it's the time for really goin' out and gettin' one of the titles."

Watts is interested in either the junior middleweight crown, currently worn by Britain's Maurice Hope, or the 160-pound championship that Vito Antuofermo is to defend next month against Marvin Hagler.

"I feel like I'd rather fight at 154 pounds because that's my natural weight," said Watts, who gave Wills a half-pound at 158½. "I wouldn't turn down a chance at the other title, though. We'll just see how things go."

Watts, once ranked among the top five 160-pounders in the world, said he and Hagler were booked to fight in Boston last February.

"They asked for a postponement until March, then cancelled because Hagler was gettin' the title shot," said Watts, who owns a disputed 1976 decision over the Brockton, Mass., boxer. "It might work out better that he cancelled because I think Marvin still has it in his mind that he'd like

to get back with me. I think he'll beat Antuofermo 'cause he's left-handed and Vito cuts, so maybe that will be the title fight for me."

Watts, whose 33-5-1 record includes only 12 fights the past five years, said he plans an intensely active two-year run for the title.

Arnold Weiss, who recently signed an agreement to book fights for Watts, is trying to place him on the undercard of next month's Victor Galindez-Marvin Johnson light-heavyweight title bout in New Orleans.

"We had about six meetings before we agreed to work together," said Weiss, who manages Johnson and Bennie Briscoe. "I told Bobby I'd only work with him as long as he held up his end. He has a history of pulling out of fights, turning down fights, demanding more money. I think now, though, he's aware there isn't time for that sort of thing."

"I turned down fights because they were offerin' guys I'd already beat," said Watts. "I lost some fights, but I never took any beatings. I wouldn't abuse my body just to make money. I'll fight anybody if I can see that it's gonna improve my situation."

"Bobby's a fine athlete, a natural talent" said Slim Perkins, who manages the fighter and trains him with Bill Folks. "He's easy to work with — always on time, takes care of business. All he needs now is some fine-tuning and the right fights."

• • •

Russell Peltz.

PUNCHLINES: Philadelphia middleweight **Boogaloo Watts** (34-5-1) fueled his comeback with a third-round knockout of **Freddie Johnson** (11-4-1), catching the New Orleans fighter with a short left uppercut. Boogaloo needs work more than he needs quick knockouts. "I'm not in the shape I want to be in yet," declared Watts. "But my legs are still good and my hands are still quick. I just want more fights. I would have liked it to go a little longer tonight" ... The Gary Hinton Bennie Gi

Joe Frazier's gym is [...]

by E.W. Faircloth

Chandler's big night
Meets Flores for NABA title

Journal photo by Mike Hill

The stars of tonight's Spectrum boxing card — Jeff Chandler (left) and Bobby (Boogaloo) Watts — ham it up at a press conference hyping the event.

Boogaloo Watts declares: 'It's time to go get a title,' after his easy victory over Clifford Wills

Watts scores TKO in third round after 11-month self-imposed layoff

FIGHTS, From 1-B

he had no complaints about the way Watts looked.

"I think it was nice," said Perkins of the quick finish. "I think it was wonderful the way he won. It's a good beginning. I hope they all end this quick.

"He needs more fights to bring his sharpness around, but the spirit is back."

Perkins, who said he had no commitments from any promoters, said he thought Watts should fight again in about six weeks. "He's still handsome," he said laughing. "He doesn't have a nick on him."

Watts was calmly happy, smiling broadly in the dressing room.

"I still have it," he said. "A couple of fights and I'll be back on top. The breaks are going to come my way and I'll get a title shot."

Richie Bennett (20-2-2) of Darby became middleweight champ of Delaware County by delivering more punishment to lefty Dan Snyder (11-11) last night than Eagles quarterback Ron Jaworski took from the Cincinnati Bengals on Sunday. He notched a TKO at 1 minute 21 seconds of the eighth round of the scheduled 10-rounder.

In other preliminaries, South Philadelphia light-heavyweight Tony Mesoroca (4-1) spoiled the pro debut of Sonny Grooms of South Philadelphia, with a TKO at 1:22 of the fourth and last round.

Middleweight Guy Gargan (11-4-5) of Upper Darby gained a split decision over Jimmie Sykes (4-2) of West Philadelphia in a six-rounder.

Middleweights Johnny Cooper of Blackwood, N.J., and Kevin Howard of North Philadelphia drew over eight rounds.

Timmy Witherspoon TKOd Joey Adams in the first round in the scheduled four-round heavyweight debut for both men.

Welterweights Bob Rooney of North Philadelphia and Xavier Biggs of South Philadelphia drew in the first pro fight for each of them.

Printed in the United States
by Baker & Taylor Publisher Services